DON'T BE A CARELESS SHOPPER!

Read this book first.
Careless shopping damages the world!
Let's follow an ordinary family on a
trip to a supermarket and find out...

how to save energy when you go shopping!

what to look for on package labels!

how to help wild animals and farm animals!

how beefburgers eat up forests!

What would you sell if you had a shop?..

LOTS OF GOODIES!?

ICE CREAM!

SWEETS!

COMICS!

TOYS!

BUT... people need other things too! For instance, what about...

FRYING PANS?

CURRY POWDER?

BEANS?

TOILET ROLLS?

You'd need a huge shop to sell everything that your customers might want!
In fact, you'd have to open

A SUPERMARKET!..

SUPA SHOP

WHAT DID YOU BUY THIS WEEK?

Lots of families do their shopping in a supermarket...

They usually take a shopping list like this...

SATURDAY — SUPERMARKET

Beefburgers
Bread
Bottled water
Hand soap
Toilet cleaner
Lemonade
Fish fingers
Chicken
Eggs
Cans of drinks
Toothpaste
Bananas

Potatoes
Spaghetti
2 tins Tuna
Melon
Pineapple
Sweetcorn
Dog food
Corned beef
cheese
Baked beans
Tea bags
Washing-up Liquid

Most shoppers buy more things than they have on their shopping lists.

Find out how many things your family buys in a week.

CHECK OUT THE CHECK-OUT!

Save up all those till receipts and see how much your family spends...

WE BUY THINGS WE NEED...

Everybody needs food and water, a home to live in, clothes to wear and good health.

FOOD AND WATER

We need good food and water to be able to live and grow.

CLOTHES AND SHELTER

We need clothes to protect us from the weather. We need homes to shelter us too.

HEALTH AND HYGIENE

We need to keep our bodies healthy to enjoy a happy life.

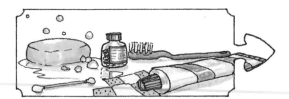

WE BUY THINGS WE LIKE...

People get bored eating plain food, wearing dull clothes and so on. They like to have a bit of variety...

FUN FOOD AND DRINK
Ordinary food made from flour, such as bread, isn't nearly as much fun to eat as spaceship-shaped macaroni!

FASHION CLOTHES
It's fashionable to be seen wearing a T-shirt from the latest adventure movie.

BEAUTIFUL HOMES
People like to make their homes look nice and clean. They buy things such as blue water dye for their toilets. It doesn't make the toilet much cleaner, but it looks pretty!

We do about half of our shopping in supermarkets...

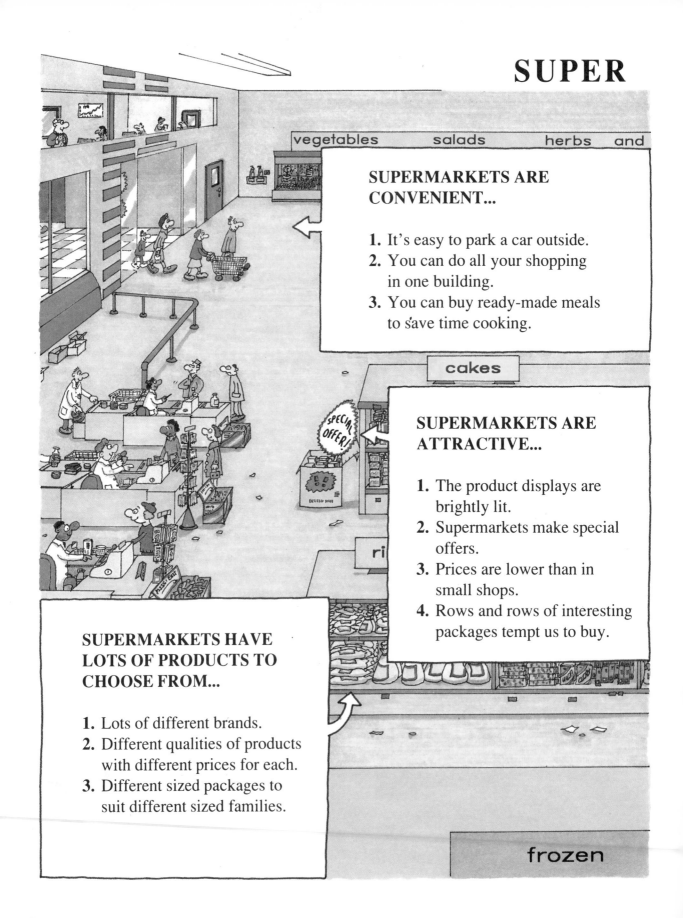

vegetables   salads   herbs   and

SUPERMARKETS ARE CONVENIENT...

1. It's easy to park a car outside.
2. You can do all your shopping in one building.
3. You can buy ready-made meals to save time cooking.

cakes

SPECIAL OFFER!

SUPERMARKETS ARE ATTRACTIVE...

1. The product displays are brightly lit.
2. Supermarkets make special offers.
3. Prices are lower than in small shops.
4. Rows and rows of interesting packages tempt us to buy.

ri

SUPERMARKETS HAVE LOTS OF PRODUCTS TO CHOOSE FROM...

1. Lots of different brands.
2. Different qualities of products with different prices for each.
3. Different sized packages to suit different sized families.

frozen

SUPERMARKETS

spices   fruit   fresh meat

SUPERMARKET SHELVES ARE USUALLY FULL...

1. You can buy the same products all the year round.
2. Big supermarkets are called hypermarkets. You can buy almost anything you can think of in a hypermarket...

SPECIAL OFFER!
ANIMAL BALLOONS

ead

flour   corn

SUPERMARKETS ARE USUALLY HYGIENIC...

1. Almost everything in a supermarket is sealed in hygienic packaging.
2. Chilled food and food for the freezer is kept cold so that it doesn't go bad too quickly.
3. Most packages have a 'sell by' date on the label. If a product isn't bought by this date, the supermarket throws it away because it might have gone bad. Some supermarkets give their 'out of date' products to charities.

food

JUNK FOOD

Supermarkets are usually hygienic.
BUT... that doesn't mean that everything they sell is good for you. What you buy is up to you!

All the displays are attractive. They can tempt us to buy the wrong sort of food.

This is sort of food is called junk food.

We can't just live on biscuits and sweets. We need to eat green vegetables, fruit and some animal products too.

AND... people who eat too much sweet or fatty food can get very fat...

FAT FACT

Not all fat people eat too much. Some people put on weight just by eating normal amounts of food. People like this have to be very careful what they eat.

Lots of cheap snacks also have **ADDITIVES** in them.

These are chemicals which food scientists add to food. Additives are used to colour food, to flavour food and to preserve food.

BUT... food makers also use additives to fool people.
Did you know that there's no chocolate in some chocolate cakes?!..

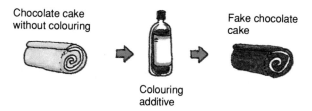

Chocolate cake without colouring → Colouring additive → Fake chocolate cake

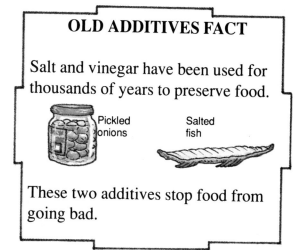

OLD ADDITIVES FACT

Salt and vinegar have been used for thousands of years to preserve food.

Pickled onions

Salted fish

These two additives stop food from going bad.

Food makers add a chemical colour such as Brown HT to make their cakes look chocolatey!

And how about those nice pink sausages? Real meat sausages are almost grey. Cheap sausages are made of fat, bread and gristle. Then a pink colour such as Red 2G is added to make them look meaty!

Nasty cheap sausage → Add a red colour → Tasty-looking sausage

SO... food scientists could easily make pink chocolate cake or even green sausages!..

CAREFUL SHOPPING GUIDE

Some additives affect the health of sensitive people. For example...

SO...

1. Always try to buy fresh food.

2. Check out package labels. Avoid fake flavours and colours when you can.

BLERRGH!

Brown HT gives some people spots.

ZZZZZ!

Red 2G makes some people feel tired.

ANIMALS AND CHEMICALS

In most countries, the law says that new additives have to be tested. This is to see if they're safe before they're used. Animals are almost always used for these tests.

ADDITIVES

A new food additive might be tried out on a pig...

BUT... it's not just additives which are tested on animals. For example...

COSMETICS

A new shampoo might be tried out on mice...

MEDICINES

New medicines are tested on animals too. Scientists first make the test animals ill by injecting them with a disease. Then they give them the new medicine.

Many of these products turn out to be harmless. BUT... some are discovered to be deadly poisons!

ANIMALS AND YOU

DOES TESTING DO
ANY GOOD??..

Chemicals injure animals and human bodies
in different ways.
So testing new products on animals doesn't
always mean that they're safe for people...

CAREFUL SHOPPING GUIDE

1. Stick to well-tried medicines and cosmetics.

2. If you have to use new products, check the labels.
   Some companies, such as The Body Shop, don't
   test their products on animals.

3. Sometimes there's no information on the label. Shop
   assistants might not know much either. Write to the
   product makers to find out if their products have
   been tested on animals.

BUT... never try to
treat yourself.

Some medicines
become poisonous
after they've been
stored for a long time.

Of course, most animals aren't
used for experiments.

THEY'RE USED FOR FOOD!..

OLD McDONALD'S FARM

"Here a quack, there a quack, everywhere a quack quack"

Everybody knows what a nursery rhyme farm looks like. Pigs, horses, chickens, sheep and cows all living together and having farmyard fun!..

BUT... these days, many farmers don't let their animals have any fun.
Animals are often tied up and fed on artificial food.
So... modern farms often look like prisons!..

Farms like these are sometimes called factory farms. They make all sorts of other animal products as well as meat.

Here are just a few of them...

Many people think it's wrong to keep animals in cages or sheds.

BUT... factory farmers say that their animals are safer and happier indoors.

WHAT DO YOU THINK??

If you decide to support old-fashioned farms, follow the...

CAREFUL SHOPPING GUIDE

1. If you buy animal products, look at the labels. "FREE RANGE" means that the animals haven't been kept in factory farms.

2. You don't need to eat meat all the time to stay healthy. Try to cut down meat-eating to once or twice a week. Vegetarians are people who don't eat meat at all.

MEAT AND WILDLIFE

Not all meat products come from factory farms.

AND... the supermarket doesn't have cows in a field round the back!

Some cattle and sheep are raised on huge open farms called..:

RANCHES

Beef cattle need a lot of open space. Cattle ranchers in Brazil cut down thousands of trees each week to clear the way for new ranches. The wild animals which live in the trees lose their homes.

So... buying too many beefburgers may damage wildlife!

CHOPPED-DOWN TREES FACT

In 1950 there were twice as many trees in the Earth's forests as there are now!

TREES AND SOIL

Trees and grass also help to stop soil from being blown or washed away. Some scientists think that the Sahara Desert was caused by sheep and goats which ate all the grass.

Parts of Australia are running out of grassland too!..

SHOCK SHEEP FACT

There are about 160 million sheep in Australia. That's ten times as many sheep as people!

Much of the meat from ranches is made into pet food.

FISH FINGERS AND FISH

Floating fish factory

Fish are one of the few sorts of wild animals which we still hunt for food. They're caught in huge nets. Floating factories turn them into fish fillets or fish fingers.

If we catch too many fish, there won't be enough left to produce more fish...

FISH LONELY HEARTS CLUB

CANNED FISH

Sometimes we buy our fish in cans. Canning stops the fish from going bad on its long trip to the supermarket. BUT... making cans uses up valuable metals such as aluminium. These metals are wasted when we throw away the empty containers.

FISH FINGERS
Fish fingers are easier to cook than fresh fish. BUT... long cold storage and additives make them lose some of their goodness.

WHALE FOOD
Most countries have stopped hunting whales because they had almost died out. Some countries have started fishing for krill. These tiny shrimp-like animals are food for some types of whales. So... if we catch too many krill, we'll still be killing whales!

Fish thumbs!

Krill
Whale

CAREFUL SHOPPING GUIDE

1. Buy fresh fish whenever possible

2. Eat fish which has been caught locally.

3. Don't be tempted by attractive packaging.

NEW! KRILSNAX

FRUIT AND VEG.

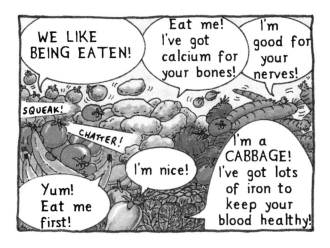

We don't just need meat products for food. We need fruit and vegetables too. They contain chemicals which our bodies need. Plants collect these chemicals from the soil. Then they pass the chemicals on to us when we eat them.

Growing too many crops can cause deserts to form.

All crops need soil to grow in and lots of water. The soil contains chemicals which the plants need too.

BUT... some farmers grow more crops than is good for the land. These extra crops use up too much water and soil chemicals.

So... farmers have to add extra water and artificial chemicals to the soil.

They also add chemicals to kill insects which might eat their crops. This poisons the soil and can injure other wildlife.

Artificial soil chemicals can poison all sorts of wildlife.

AND... these chemicals can soak into our drinking water!..

Bottled water is nearly always safe to drink.

16

BUYING ORGANIC

Farmers who don't use artificial chemicals are called organic farmers.

They look after the soil by not growing too many plants.

And... organic crops are good for us too. We need the right amounts of soil chemicals in the plants we eat so as to stay healthy.

CAREFUL SHOPPING GUIDE

1. Get your parents to buy organic food when they can. Look for labels in greengrocers. Organic crops may cost a little more but it's worth it to protect your health.

2. If you've got a garden, try growing your own crops!

Not all crops are used for food.
For example...

COTTON

Cotton is a crop which needs an enormous amount of water to grow. If you buy any cotton clothes, look after them. They will have cost the world a lot of water to make.

INCREDIBLE SHRINKING SEA FACT

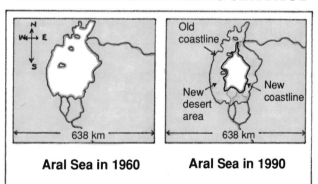

Aral Sea in 1960   **Aral Sea in 1990**

The Aral Sea is in the USSR. Rivers which flow into it have been used to water huge cotton fields. This has shrunk this sea and turned its coastline into deserts!

DIGGING FOR TOOTHPASTE!

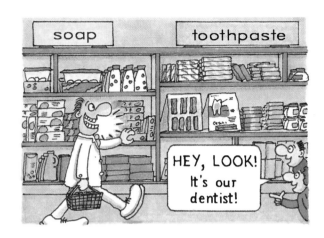

Of course, we don't just go shopping for food. We also buy non-food items such as toothpaste, soap, teapots and lawn-mowers. These sorts of things are made from raw materials dug from the ground.

People even dig for toothpaste!..

"TOOTHPASTE MINE" FACT

A mountain of waste like this is called a spoil heap.

TOOTHPASTE TOOTHBRUSH ~ AND CUP ~ SPECIAL OFFER!

Toothpaste is made of a fine white clay called china clay. Water and other chemicals are added before it's packed into tubes. China clay is also used to make pottery.

We have to shift a lot of rock and soil to get at most raw materials. So after years of digging, ugly piles of waste build up.

BUT... there isn't an endless supply of raw materials. Take coal for example...

COAL HOLE FACT

Looks like we're lost again, Bert!

Coal is one of the raw materials used to make medicines, dyes and clothes. Some experts think we'll run out of coal in another two hundred years. Coal is getting hard to find even now!..

OIL ABOARD!

You can buy car oil in many supermarkets.
Lots of things such as plastic are made of oil too.

Oil is taken from the ground - from oil wells. Then it's shipped all over the world in huge tankers.
AND... accidents will happen!..

BUT THAT'S NOT ALL!..

Factories use energy to turn raw materials into products. Power stations supply this energy by burning coal, oil or gas.
These burning fuels pollute the air with millions of tonnes of waste gases.
So... the more products we buy or waste...

- **The more raw materials we dig up!**
- **The more energy we use!**
- **The more we damage the environment!**

OILY BIRDS AND FISH FACT

In 1989, the tanker *Exxon Valdez* ran aground in Alaska. Fifty million litres of crude oil spilled into the sea.

CAREFUL SHOPPING GUIDE

You can help to solve these problems by careful shopping!

1. Buy longer-lasting products...

2. Don't waste them or misuse them...

3. Don't throw anything away before it's worn out.

WHAT'S PACKAGING FOR?..

Most of the things on supermarket shelves are packed in boxes, bottles, jars and cans.

This packaging makes shopping easier for customers and shopkeepers.

1. KEEPING STUFF IN

Most food products need some sort of packaging. Think what it would be like taking home loose jam!..

2. PORTION CONTROL

Years ago, all food was sold loose. The shopkeeper had to weigh products and pack bags for each customer.

Shopping is quicker these days. Carefully measured portions are pre-packed before they're sent to the shops.

BUT... that means you sometimes have to buy more than you need!..

3. HYGIENE

Modern packaging helps to keep food fresh. Take corned beef for example. When it's made, it's packed into cans. Then it's heated up to kill off any bacteria it may contain. Cans of corned beef can be eaten after being stored for years!

...AND WHAT'S IT MADE OF?

Just like everything else we buy, packaging is made from raw materials.

1. GLASS

Glass is made by mixing and heating limestone, soda and sand. There are plenty of these raw materials.
BUT... it takes a lot of energy to turn them into glass. Some shops sell drinks in returnable glass bottles. These are refilled and used again and again.
So returnable bottles save our energy!

2. PLASTIC

Most plastics are made from oil. Some scientists say we'll run out of oil by the year 2020. The more plastic we buy and throw away, the sooner we'll run out of oil!

3. METAL

Cans are made of steel or aluminium. Two million tonnes of aluminium are used every year for packaging!

4. PAPER AND CARDBOARD

Take a look in your dustbin. Most of your rubbish is paper and cardboard packaging. Much of this is made of wood from trees!

An average tree makes 13 tonnes of waste paper.

LOADSARUBBISH!

Some product makers go completely mad with their packaging!..

HOW ABOUT A NICE CUP OF TEA?

Tea leaves

Tea leaves packed into a dunking bag

Tea leaves in a dunking bag with a fancy stapled label

Individual sachet for dunking bag of tea leaves with a fancy stapled label

Box for twenty-four individual sachets of dunking bags of tea leaves with fancy stapled labels

Free fold-out guide to making the best of your box of tea leaves in dunking bags with fancy stapled labels in twenty-four individual sachets

...and plastic wrapping round all of it!

When shoppers buy products, they have to buy the packaging too. Half the cost of some products is just for the packaging!

BUT... not only do we pay for the packaging, we pay to get rid of it too.

Rubbish is either dumped or burned. Dumping uses up valuable land and pollutes the soil and the sea. Burning rubbish pollutes the air.

TRY THIS TONGUE TWISTER...
PLASTIC PACKAGES POSE PROBLEMS, PUMP UP PRICES AND PRODUCE POLLUTION!

ERK!

TO THE SIMPLE PACKAGING SHOP

Some shops sell loose products such as herbs, coffee, sweets and tea in simple paper bags. These bags are cheap and can be used again.

environment friendly washing-up liquid

Look out for biodegradable carrier-bags!

LESS RUBBISH!

Most of the rubbish we dump rots away in the ground. Bacteria in the soil break it down by eating it. But... most plastics don't rot away because bacteria can't eat them.

When a product or its packaging can be eaten by bacteria, it's called biodegradable. Look out for products and containers labelled as biodegradable.

We waste our money and the world's raw materials by throwing old packaging away. BUT... we can use some containers over and over again. This is called recycling.

Find out how to cut down on waste by recycling. You can recycle...

- glass bottles and jars
- paper and cardboard
- metal cans
- and lots more!

RUSSIAN PACKAGE FACT

At the *GOM* supermarket in Moscow, products aren't always packaged. Shoppers can buy packaging at another shop.

УПАКОВКА МАГАЗИН

CAREFUL SHOPPING GUIDE

1. Buy returnable bottles and cans. Try to avoid plastic containers.

2. Go for simple, cheap packaging.

3. Look for biodegradable products and packaging.

MUNCH!! SLURP!! YUM YUM! HUNGRY BACTERIA

4. Find out which local shops will let you bring your own containers.

5. Try to find ways to recycle used packaging...

BEANS

HOW TO PLAY

1. You need a drawing of a shopping trolley on a small piece of card for each player.

2. Use a dice. Each player throws the dice in turn. The first to throw a six starts the game.

3. Follow the rules written on the squares. The first player to get to the exit is the winner.

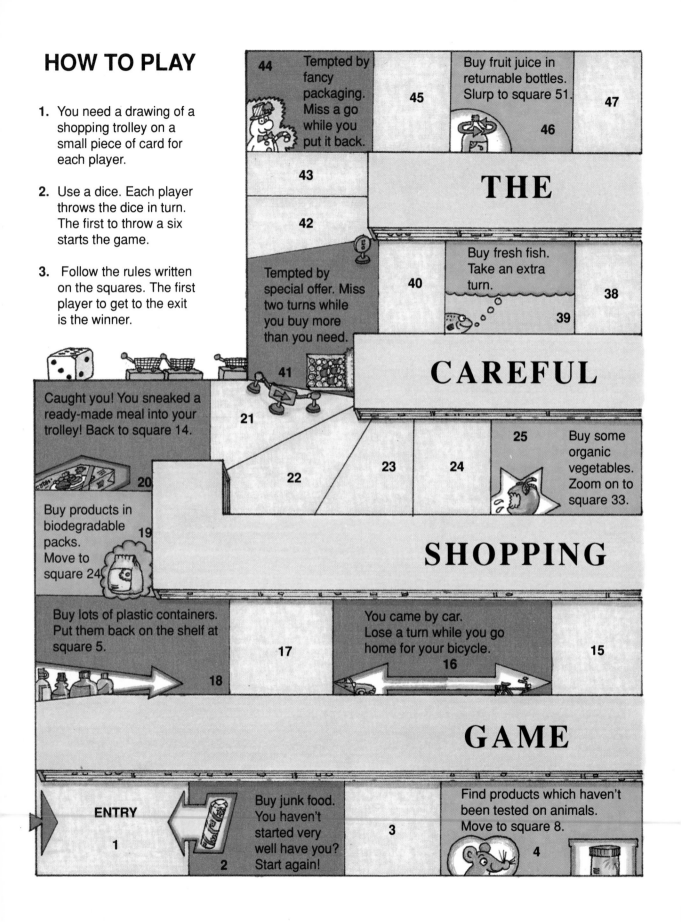

44 Tempted by fancy packaging. Miss a go while you put it back.

45

Buy fruit juice in returnable bottles. Slurp to square 51.

47

46

43

42

THE

40

Buy fresh fish. Take an extra turn.

38

39

Tempted by special offer. Miss two turns while you buy more than you need.

41

CAREFUL

Caught you! You sneaked a ready-made meal into your trolley! Back to square 14.

21

22

23

24

25 Buy some organic vegetables. Zoom on to square 33.

20

Buy products in biodegradable packs. Move to square 24.

19

SHOPPING

Buy lots of plastic containers. Put them back on the shelf at square 5.

18

17

You came by car. Lose a turn while you go home for your bicycle.

16

15

GAME

ENTRY

1

Buy junk food. You haven't started very well have you? Start again!

2

3

Find products which haven't been tested on animals. Move to square 8.

4

24

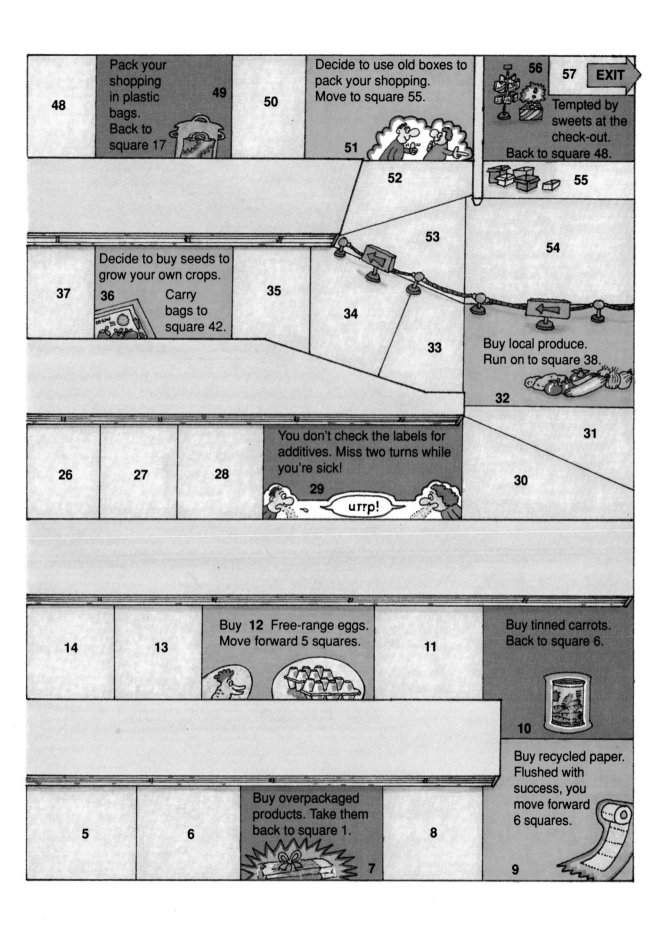

48

49 Pack your shopping in plastic bags. Back to square 17

50

51 Decide to use old boxes to pack your shopping. Move to square 55.

52

56

57 EXIT

Tempted by sweets at the check-out. Back to square 48.

55

37

36 Decide to buy seeds to grow your own crops. Carry bags to square 42.

35

34

53

54

33

32 Buy local produce. Run on to square 38.

31

26

27

28

29 You don't check the labels for additives. Miss two turns while you're sick!

urrp!

30

14

13

12 Buy Free-range eggs. Move forward 5 squares.

11

10 Buy tinned carrots. Back to square 6.

5

6

7 Buy overpackaged products. Take them back to square 1.

8

9 Buy recycled paper. Flushed with success, you move forward 6 squares.

25

ON THE ROAD

Most big supermarkets are built outside towns.

They're designed for people with cars. People without cars have to manage as best they can...

The more we use cars for shopping, the more pollution and accidents there are!

All the items we buy in supermarkets are brought by trucks or vans. There are about one hundred million delivery vehicles on the world's roads.
They all use petrol or diesel fuel and give off smoky waste gases.

OFF THE ROAD

Aeroplanes and ships bring products from around the world. Many of these items could be produced locally. Needlessly transporting stuff from thousands of miles away is a waste of fuel and raw materials!

CAREFUL SHOPPING GUIDE

1. Do your shopping near where you live. Using local shops helps them to stay in business. Local shops are better for poor, disabled or old people who might not have a car.

2. Don't go shopping by car if you don't need to. Use public transport, or walk or cycle to the shops.

3. Look at the labels on products. Try to buy things which have been made or grown near to where you live.

Nowadays we eat and use products from all over the world without thinking much about it.

Find out about THE AMAZING WORLD OF DINNERS! See if you can do the...

COOK'S TOUR QUIZ!

Each of the items in this dining room come from different countries. Can you find the countries on the map?

Potatoes - Egypt

Spaghetti - Italy

Tuna fish - Fiji

Melon - Paraguay

Wheat bread - Canada

Pineapple - Philippines

Sweetcorn - U.S.A.

Bananas - Surinam

Plates - Taiwan

T.V. - Japan

Baked beans - Mexico

Table cloth Eire

Cheese - Holland

Corned beef - Kenya

T.V. show - Australia

Glasses - Denmark

Dog food beef - Argentina
Dog food Soya - China

Chairs - Brazil

Table mats - Sri Lanka

Cutlery - South Korea

AFTER DINNER HINTS

WASHING UP

Old fashioned washing-up liquids aren't always biodegradable.

Some new types are. But... they still come in plastic containers, so they waste raw materials.

Some shops sell big blocks of washing-up soap. These clean more dishes for your money - and there's no waste!

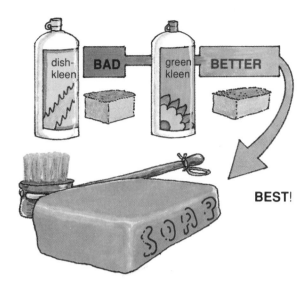

TIDYING UP

Some people have more than one dustbin.

BUT... they're not being greedy - they're being careful!

Why not try to split up your "rubbish" like this?..

COMPOST BIN	METAL BIN	GLASS BIN	PAPER BIN	RUBBISH BIN
For vegetable scraps. These can be saved in the bin until bacteria have biodegraded them. This produces compost which can be spread on the garden to help plants to grow.	For bottle tops, cans and so on. Scrap metal merchants take old metal for recycling.	For bottles and jars. Most of these aren't returnable. BUT... you can save them and take them to a bottle bank for recycling.	For clean paper and cardboard. Find out if there's a paper merchant near you who'll collect your old paper.	For general rubbish. Careful shopping means this bin doesn't have to be emptied very often!

TTER LITTER LITTER LITTER LIT

SOME DIRTY PEOPLE USE THE STREETS AS DUSTBINS

Have you ever thrown a sweet wrapper away? It's not really litter is it?
It's only a small piece of paper or plastic...
BUT... what would happen if everybody thought like that?

If we all put our rubbish into the streets and parks, the world would look like this!..

WEMBLEY LITTER FACT

Every year at the English FA Cup Final at Wembley, the crowd drops twenty tonnes of litter!

LEAF LITTER
Sweeping streets and parks costs a huge amount of money. If everybody looked after the environment, we would only need to sweep up fallen leaves.

LITTER OF THE LAW
Litter could be expensive for you too. In most countries, you can be fined for dropping litter.

TER LITTER LITTER LITTER LITT

And... litter can be dangerous too!..

A DANGEROUS NEWSPAPER

A DANGEROUS BOTTLE

DANGEROUS BUBBLE GUM
(AND OTHER THINGS!)

CAREFUL LITTER GUIDE!

You can help to keep our planet
clean and tidy...

1. Most litter is found near shops.
   Ask your local sweet-shop
   owner to put a bin outside the
   shop.

2. Get your teacher to organise
   litter pick-up squads at your
   school!

Careless shopping ruins the world for everybody.
Now that you've read this book, you'll know that careful shopping helps to keep our planet safe and healthy.

BUY LESS NOW...

AND SAVE THE WORLD LATER!

INDEX